BUSHWICK POETRY

RABBLE ROUSE THE WORLD

BOOKS

A Division of Rabble Rouse The World LLC
Bushwick 2013
RabbleRouseTheWorld.com

Bushwick Poetry

Edited by Luke Maguire Armstrong

Bushwick Poetry

Rabble Rouse The World Press
www.RabbleRouseTheWorld.com
Rabble@RabbleRouseTheWorld.com
@RRTW

For information about special discounts for bulk purchases, readings or Irish jigs please contact the email listed above.

ISBN-13: 978-0615886381

ISBN-10: 0615886388

Editor Bio

Luke Maguire Armstrong (TravelWriteSing.Com) was a baby, who became a boy, who became a man who wrote music and words. Once he fought a bear and almost died. Haters later claimed it was "only a raccoon" and he was acting like "a little girl."

Luke has spent the last five years working in human rights, education and development from Guatemala to Kenya to The Bronx. He moved to Bushwick October, 2012. He is the author of four books, including "iPoems for the Dolphins to Click Home About" and "How We Are Human." @LukeSpartacus

Author Bios

Alan Charnock is a writer from Texas currently living  in Bushwick. He writes essays, plays, and poetry; works for the You Heard It Here First podcast; and is part of CommonCompany.org. @ABCharnock.

Aebra Coe is a native of Michigan and graduate of the  University of Michigan, but calls Ridgewood home. She can be found most evenings unwinding from a day job in journalism by tramping through the streets of Bushwick with her bear-like and exuberant golden retriever, Milo.

Samuel DiBella (DeadLetterOffC.Tumblr.com) is a student at NYU and President of The Headless Writer's Society. He is originally from Rhode Island.

Gary Estanislao lives in New York and cooks for a living—and writes, paints, gardens. He had taught grade school and high school, beginning in Portland, OR. He has an intelligent dog named Jung. And they live in Bushwick, Brooklyn.

Jonathan Zuckerman is a writer/musician from Queens. He's lived in Brooklyn for the past two years. You've probably seen him on the train.

Patricia E. Gillespie is the daughter of a union man and  a painter. She's been trying to live that down since 1989. Born in the fair suburb of Yonkers, NY and raised not far from a New England diaper factory, she tries not to live too far from the Hudson River. She was published in a few internet magazines you've never heard of. She also makes movies you might be able to Google.

Aaron Rush Hicks moved to New York to become a  vegan chef. He had no idea the wild ride the city had in store for him. Today he is a fire breathing, contortionist, sword swallowing clown (often a naked one). By night you can find him performing everywhere from The Goodbye Blue Monday, Bizarre Bar, to your backyard, or his day job, the Coney Island freak show.

Erica Jane was raised in Grosse Pointe, Michigan. After

 receiving her B.A. in 2012, she moved to Bushwick with a suitcase, a résumé , and a small stack of books. She has been happy ever since.

Julianne Mason is a singer/songwriter and musician.

 She is a graduate of the University of Northern Iowa and originally from Marshalltown, Iowa. She now resides happily in New York City with her two beautiful daughters, Zoe and Bea.

Arthur Manuel Medrano is a poet and a musician who

 was born and raised in New York City. He has been writing poetry since the age of 16. He studied Liberal Arts at Kingsborough Community College and currently is studying Creative Writing at Brooklyn College.

Brittany Natale is a modern-day Renaissance woman who was born and raised in Queens and now lives in

 Brooklyn. She currently works at the Williamsburg Art & Historical Center and sometimes writes for Bushwick Daily. She enjoys exploring, secondhand shops, psychology books, and sunshine and lives by the Gandhi idea "be the change you wish to see in the world".

Kia Ochun just moved to Bushwick from New Orleans.

She is originally from Washington State. Most days you can find her planing her banjo on the streets most. She moved to Bushwick to build instruments at the Jalopy Theatre.

Linda Penny is a frequent face around Bushwick. I first

met her at the Goodbye Blue Monday on Broadway. She raised five kids to adulthood and to those who know her, we call her mom, even though she swears like a pirate. Meet her at a bar and if you're lucky she might just take out her iPad and share a poem with you. She is a kindred spirit with a warm heart who shockingly enough, only began writing poetry late last year. This book is the first time her work has been formerly published. *-Ed.*

Tami O'Neill is a copywriter, editor and product of the

NYC public school system. She has been frantically scribbling short stories and general musings in Mead notebooks, Wordpad files and on the back of old receipts since learning what a slant rhyme was at age 9. This is her first submission for publication, with more works on the horizon. In the meantime, Tami can be found at various day jobs trying to meet Bushwick's ever-increasing rent prices.

Paul Raphaelson has lived in Bushwick since 2004.

Known primarily as a photographic artist, he has lately become curious about what language can do when provoked. Some of his current experiments involve text combined with images. His more successful experiments involve food. PaulRaphaelson.com.

Amy Richards grew up on Long Island, with the

dream of one day living in Bushwick. She is a social justice advocate and educator, working with youth and NY's Latino immigrant community. Currently, she is fulfilling a Fulbright year in Bogota, Colombia, where she is part of a number of initiatives for achieving peace and reconciliation through creative expression and civic leadership. She is busy helping translate poetry, climbing things, and surviving the daily commute on Bogota's public bus system, the Transmilenio.

Table of Contents

FORWARD

I know it was late because when I went inside to use the bathroom the last act of the night at The Goodbye Blue Monday was packing up their instruments. I invited the musicians to come out back and they joined our circle of patio chair.

Half of us had instruments in our hands. We were going around the circle, singing songs and reciting memorized or made-up poetry. Bushwickeans, or Bushwackers—whatever you call this undercurrent of artists around here who sway to verses, clink their $3 pints of PBR, laugh in elation, wield words like weapons, slap backs and high-fives into hands, free-style, mix poetry with music, music with art and art with life.

Nights like this abound in Bushwick. I moved to New York for the usual reasons—to pursue artistic endeavors with like minded people who never asked why you were doing what you did.

I went to the "important" Manhattan poetry events and readings, at such hold-steady places like the KGB Bar on the Lower East Side and events off Union Square sponsored by P&Ws. I enjoyed my time listening to those considered the top US poets, but that poetry often felt as static as and lifeless as Biblical texts compared to the what was happening in Bushwick.

Bushwick was the New York I came searching for —Kerouac and Ginsberg's New York. In Bushwick they were not just reading poetry, they were living poetic lives and this shone with a different shimmer than the ivory tower keepers of verse. Here it is not uncommon to find yourself at a table consisting of sculptors, painters, performers, clowns, fire-breathers, sword swallowers, actors, film makers, and once, a guinea pig.

A half dozen PBRs deep and inhaling a communal spliff, I decided on a night late in May in the back of The Goodbye Blue Monday that I would endeavor to herd the verses of these poetic cats onto the same page and put together an anthology capturing the moment of Bushwick that I reveled in nightly.

The result is the book in your hands or on your device. I put out the word in the usual way—putting up flyers, throwing an ad in the Bushwick Daily, and putting out feelers in Bushwick's powerful word of mouth. I had no idea what would come my way, but was not disappointed with the collection of reaching verse that accumulated in my inbox.

While these may not sing the full song of Bushwick, it certainly tells the tale of the current influx of today's gentrification, and explores their lives and longings while putting on display the communal thread uniting this newish sect of current gentrifiers.

Bushwick has a long history of changing demographies. Ever since Peter Stuyvesant named the area *Boswijck* (little town in the woods) in 1661, Bushwick has been in a racial and economic flux. We humbly remind Williamsburg that it was once a part of *Boswijck*.

A one paragraph summery of a four hundred year history can only say that the many faces of Bushwicks past have included contested territory fought between Colonists screwing Native Americans out of their land, the 1840s and 1850s when Germans started arriving en masse, the 1890s when it became a hub of breweries, Prohibition when Bushwick underwent an economic boom (bootlegging anyone?), the 1950s when Bushwick was one of the largest Italian/American neighborhoods, the 70s, 80s and 90s when Bushwick was defined by empty lots, crime, poverty, drugs and arson.

Today Bushwick is mostly Hispanic with the cheap NYC rents that inevitably invites the surfeit of the hungry artists.

Bushwick Poetry is the communal account of bursting hearts reaching for transcendental vibes of artistic elation. These are the stories of fleeting moments, following dreams, side-walk busking, breaking and healing hearts, late night reflections in the rain, walking alone in a city of eight million people and finding community in the glances of late night subway cars.

This collection includes verse from poets like Patricia Gillespie whose poetry pokes at something familiar with potent lines that seem to alternate between hard hits and shared intimacy. Her poetry feels like a much needed sharing with a close friend during a slow brunch outside of normal New York quicktime.

"I want you to ask questions. / Questions you have answers to," This encapsulates something timeless about our generation, of wanting tangible answers to questions, not religious dogma.

In Bushwick Poetry Erica Jane is " Unperturbed / by the stirrings of strangers / scattered in diagonal chairs / under the eyelid of night," and Tami O'Neil reminds us that "If ever you're in need of someone to talk to / simply light a cigarette in front of Pennsylvania Station."

Aaron Rush Hicks wonders if "I am the only man with no place to be?" Linda Penny claims "[she] knows you" and asks directly, "Does your hungry soul suffer so? . . . Did you feast on my fear?"

Lights on broadway seem to shout to Alan Charnock to "get out, get out of the gathering gloom." There is a big city darkness throughout the verse, but the sort of tenebrosity that comes from seeking out, demanding brilliantly bright light.

Julianne Mason has "Quiet streets that [she] cannot cross," and Amy Richards "tore [her] shirt into a hundred pieces / wanting to bury [her] head in it." Together the poems relate a silver lining of hope we expect from youthful artists spending their days and nights in a city that has always enchanted and attracted such a sect.

Aebra Coe is "Smiling at the Myrtle Ave. sign, / the bodega cat,/the rainbow of shoes that cross the street" and Paul Raphaelson thinks that "You look like nice people. [He'll] give you a lemon wedge" while Arthur Medrano still wants to believe in the tragic magic. . . from which he draws grace.

-Luke Maguire Armstrong

Bushwick Poetry

I love these women of Bushwick.

~ Linda Penny

Bushwick Poetry

These Beauties of Bushwick
Linda Penny

I love these women of Bushwick. The soft cheek against mine in greeting. Hello love. Sweet dreams of a light caress in crisp, cool white sheets, growing warm, falling, floating, gentle upon her skin. These sweet lovely warm women of Bushwick. Nestled in my arms, that touch, that stroke, that hunger. Sweet breath across my face calling me back to delicate smiles and soft eyes on a candle-lit night. Oh, how I love these women of Bushwick.

She brought me a drink once, in a garden, once, her scent so sweet, so sweet. The wine was rosy red and I drank deep and hard. I drank, and still, I thirst for more. I thirst for these beauties, these gentle beauties, these beautiful women of Bushwick.

An Optimist's Afternoon

Aebra Coe

Smiling at the Myrtle Ave. sign,
the bodega cat,
the rainbow of shoes that cross the street.

Nodding at John Paul who
forever peers toward heaven.

Winking at the little lady
who cries into her phone,
"Don't go. Don't go."

The movement of the city
on an optimist's afternoon,
all the beautiful women walk their dogs.

Since the worst thing that could happen
has
nothing worries me anymore.

Smiles splatter like buckshot
on the concrete,
rain gurgles in the gutter.

Alyssa, I Apologize for Inviting You to the Secret Meeting

Paul Raphaelson

Offering apple juice for the axial, integral moment
in cultural evolution, our host won't hold court, holds rather
many records. Retires. Ideas lack requisite swiftness, we
creep, blind mechanics probing the engine. Timing light:
quantify speed with what shimmers still as its ghost.

There is no wine, you notice

but on the Japanese wall, megalithic hi-fi, bears
rebuilt mid-non-menacing stride, by the Nazi
battleship preserved in lucite, racing helmet, collection
of collections marshaled expensively, sharing outlets.

The engine is talk.

White bearded men smell like 1967. Association, smoke,
a low carbon footprint potluck, now strategies for torquing
the world toward a pre-imagined arousal: *It's like the*
shamanistic ritual by which we regress chemically
for the purpose of knowing — yes, like the earth's wobble corrupting
the Babylonian zodiac. I mean, just like the noosphere and the
proposition by the French paleontologist of the one consciousness,
that suffering due to total collapse will be mitigated by the sheer
redundancy of suffering.

Perhaps we are dreamed by the Prussian gatling gun
by the sewing machine.

Sounds of argument: Gaia vs. universal broadband, sucking
attention from the door. Your fingernails impress my thigh.

Run. Thank the Goddess for the out, the Thai restaurant
happy hour. Well drinks $4. Hot toddy for the rawness?
you ask. *For 4 I can make it with vodka, soda, ice.*
You look like nice people. I'll give you a lemon wedge.

And the audience loves you
Erica Jane

Grand plans
for the upcoming feature
starring you
and me too.
Some people think I'm the lead
but you have close-ups
And the audience loves you
for the glint in your eyes
and the occasional clumsiness
that turns stunning beauty
into something
to be savored.
Trying to avoid you
to think of other things,
the film rolls back to you
like the cliché we recognize
and adore.
The day is lame
anticipating the night
when the air will change
and you will appear.
My memory of you

Is not you
but I carry it with me
mocking the strangers
who could never guess
what's going on.
In the end,
it will be night.
As long as the day persists,
I wait.
My memory of you
is a movie of a movie.

100 tiles

on the floor square
room on Piedmont Ave.

lady on the cot
talks about symmetry
offers me an acorn

In a three-player game of Scrabble
everyone finds GOD, she says,

Or symmetry, I reply; it all
started with ACORN,
from the center, radial
14 points, double word score.
We are not OF this place, 2 points
Just using up my letters
she SAYS

Just trying to make words out of nothing,
I SAY, add it to the last S for
4 points, a square, an acorn
I'm winning.

-*Amy Richards*

Constellations

Jonathan Zuckerman

I've got constellations
all over my body.
My consolation prize
for freedom
For living in a place I can
afford-just barely
For sleeping in a bed
I just barely fit in
where I toss
and turn
and wake up sweating
and roll over again.

I am the great bear
clawing and pawing
constantly.
I've got the Pleiades
around my ankles, up to my knees
and the second my shoes
come off
they itch to high heavens.
Orion's Belt is under mine

on my waist,
a dotted line.

My arms have beautiful patterns
that nobody looks at
and everyone turns away from.
I'm marked
so when people see me they go,
"There's someone who's doing
something wrong."

A hundred tiny mouths
always biting
when one stops
another starts.
No way to stop it.
I glow bright red
like the night sky.
I've got constellations
all over my body.
My consolation prize.

Sky Town

Erica Jane

Unperturbed
by the stirrings of strangers
scattered in diagonal chairs
under the eyelid of night.
My back was bent
to hold your words
and I forgot the day,
this day.
How it wouldn't last forever
like I thought it would.

Untitled

Tami O'Neill

If ever you're in need of someone to talk to

simply light a cigarette in front of Pennsylvania Station.

Watch as the masses descend from thin air

to share their stories and call you 'precious honeychile'.

To bum a spare

and maybe a light

and maybe a dollar, if you have one please.

Because they're all stranded. Every last one.

And don't you know that dollar, well

that's the last one they need

to buy that golden ticket home.

And after praising your sweet, beautiful soul

they'll leave you be with a glimpse of another life

and maybe half a pack.

If you manage to last the whole fifteen minute fix

without retreating into the popcorn-scented underground

then you may just be a saint.

And if you leave the experience still craving the embrace of humanity

perhaps you are a masochist.

Three-Peaks Clouds

Gary Estanislao

Three-peaks clouds
Subtend north-facing
Morgan Avenue
Kitty cornering the lofts
Not sunset yet
Seeing the triangles from one side

This happened when
Brooklyn was a new sea
Was sailing from
At the lookout
On this building ship

Manhattan to the west
An oil tanker
Or a floating drill rig
But no longer
Off the coast of Santa Barbara

Drove up there
On weekends
To the Yellow House

Were best friends then
New to love

That was twenty years ago
And still together
Los Angeles, Portland,
Bushwick, Brooklyn
The high points of our life

We've met before.

Linda Penny

There's a crow in flight. Blue black wings, this
harbinger, this omen.
Evil on the wind.

Bring yourself to me, little bird.
Look at me here, now.
We've met before.
I know you.

I had forgotten those soft summer days.
Would you steal away the grace of a childhood
memory? Does your hungry soul suffer so?

I loved him with a fire so fierce it burned us both. Did
you feed on my passion? My loss? My pain?

Bring yourself to me. Little bird. We've met before.

When the chill of autumn wrapped me in hopes of that
one thundering storm, come bird, did you think I was
afraid? Did you go hungry that day?

When he beat me and I crawled away, did I hear your voice? Were you the one? That whisper in his ear? Did you feast on my fear?

I know you.

Come here to me little bird.
Come to me . See me now. We've met before

Come.

street sleet lovingly

Arthur Medrano

you and i, we surpass the cracked pavement.
  we walk past the shit-stained streets
  and we meet the half-acquainted disbelief
  that attracted you to me.
and i'm still passing the spots we shared -
  the caring memories we had and cherished
  in place of the constructed exiles we've exposed.
i still want to believe in us -
  the tragic magic, your disposition and the grain,
  they all painted a picture from which i drew grace.

  i commanded the powers that be to let me be with you,
but they chose my future without you.
  a saddened puppy i exist,
  chasing the inescapable.
but you and i were attached to the hip,
  and we skipped past all the dead pools.
occasionally, we stepped in puddles of water
  that breathed life into our soles,
  but that was intended or so you think.
when i spit sometimes, it may hit you
  but don't run away if it hits your face -

it's just the loving dribble you've inspired.
and now i look for fireflies
 to get one to catch your eye
  and guide you through the darkness
 and into my whole.

Transit

Paul Raphaelson

Fingertips,
depth perception
sting with electrical potential,
I fell in love a little over coffee
without touching a thing. So it's probably real.
The internet is beautiful tonight.
Why this presentiment of hydrants opened
entirely out of season? O espionage—you
are the inappropriate touch of the muse.
A couple Brooklyn-bound on the F kissing
with all that hand sanitizer, as if to say yes
but no. To the sheer scale of his double Windsor
I am suppressing violence. My coffee was not especially delicious.
You people. Everyone eyeing me, daggers of online-date
in your unspoken monologues precisely of the historical moment,
but it was me alone, a cup marked gigantesco, not quite
      the smallest,
a page like this most decidedly not this, lost now and no
      longer needed.

Bushwick Poetry

*It's the last way ever
I loved you, whole-hearted, with no
tears.*

~ Alan Charnock

Bushwick Poetry

Dear G-d,

Aaron Rush Hicks - AKA, The Naked Clown

This memory haunts my every dream, but somehow seems wanted. Drinking one night to stop this lucid dream and going sober again to have it. Can looking backwards be looking forward? Don't things exist only in the opposition of themselves? I am a time traveler without a time machine. Damn it! I need my time machine! I need to oppose myself. Is this a rant? . . .It feels like a rant. But I can't help but think about how the last fourteen billion years have culminated to create the present moment and how perfect that is; and how if I had the chance would change it. Would I be willing to fuck with perfection, the universe to change this? Yes…. Yes I would. Give me a black hole with a 50% chance of time travel and a 50% chance of being crushed into dark matter and see if I don't jump into it! I await your response.

Lonely human,

Rush Hicks

Bad Ode on Love Games

Alan Charnock

My friends invaded Vegas and swatted
terrorists with pixelated AKs
grenading slot machines while I prepared
to drive to you and break up because
I knew you couldn't drive anywhere after
we ripped out each other's controllers
and trashed our hard drives. It's the last way I ever
I loved you, whole-hearted, with no tears.

If that was love the bonus round was hell:
wandering no sleep and barefoot into
frozen four a.m. parking lots to howl
at car alarms; interrogating you,
me, God for clues; mashing the buttons
of self-pity, drinks, heartbreak and depression,
then driving slow and drunk with my sad friends
blasting bad jazz in clownish procession
until I let go of the wheel and jumped—

You explained the 8-bit paradox that one hour with you
        could be all eternity
that one kiss could be the whole world and nothing that
this could be the glorious roll-credits end of the game
we'd been playing—
and then it didn't matter anyway

I couldn't respawn after ditching the van
had no health points or power-ups, just pain
some scrapes, and a new life which began
in an unspectacular crash of rain.
Years later I work to pay my rent
in a dim downtown and remember this
while spectral rain falls with forceful bent
on a wrinkled water tower to kiss
the city's lips and splash into mists
swept away by wind like the footsteps
of lost ghosts into the streets below
which if they froze would be shaped like snow.

Learning to Count
Amy Richards

I remember when my sister snuck into my bed and
asked if I knew what fingering was. I said it was
numbers you mark on music to show which piano keys
you hit. Sort of, she said; it was summer.

Beauty School

Erica Jane

Inside a beauty school
with clamshell walls
and rubber hands,
time passes in the sounds
of pop songs
and aluminum foil.
You trust someone
you don't know,
loosening the grip once held
around the strands.

You remember the money
the machine gave you
and you can't decide
if you're rich
or you're poor.

Under the crinkling and the heat
of your animal blanket
you remember,
there's a video somewhere
of a first haircut

with crackers in your hands
and the mirror reflected a million versions
of a world stacked upon itself.
You don't remember the memory
but you remember the video.

Now here you are,
among plastic heads
trying to be better than you were
before.

YAZ

Amy Richards

day 19 popped through its packaging
like the almost-Christmas
chocolate in an advent calendar

you could hang me like an ornament
from my tampon string
if I could only do a split
were flexible like a Nuvaring

is likely to increase your risk
of heart attack, stroke,
breast and cervical cancer

the size of an apple
on your ovary
just like growing pains
she said wielding the dildo-camera
in her white lab coat

another trans-vaginal sonogram
to poke my hemorrhagic ovarian cyst

I blacked out from the explosion

but after 2,738 days of hormones
913 placebos like candy buttons on paper tape

I am supercharged:
automatic.

Burning Down the Years

Alan Charnock

A flash of a burning house and sparks in the sky
Burn into the brain a picture of your hair
The sparks tracing strands of fire as they fall
Or fly upwards to wink at the stars in the air

But this conflagration will burn to the dirt
The dying stars recall all their rambling light
And this picture will fall from the wall of memory
It won't matter by then that your hair is turned white

So why capture this quickly fading moment from years ago
For a girl who once shook flames from her golden hair
With the wild prodigality of a prairie-fire
But who could now be anyone, anywhere?

Portland Brooklyn

Gary Estanislao

~For Karen~

Renoir said that colors, not lines
Structure the painting; that pain ends

Not beauty;
that all his
life wanted
To paint like
a child
without
thinking.

Empty
Thames St.

is raining
Gentle like Portland's complexion;
The murals have more their nature
That I've ever seen.

One of Those Nights

Jonathan Zuckerman

It's one of those nights
when the chill is comforting
when the air is like a pillow
when vibrations shoot across the bar.
It's one of those nights
when your boot heels hit the concrete
in just the right spots
when you can sit still
as eyes fall on you.
It's one of those nights
when you know there's bad
but the good is a blanket
that covers you.
It's one of those nights
when you're pregnant with poetry.
My mind is poisoned with ideas.

Whitewashed minds

Aaron Rush Hicks

Walking the dark and damp streets of New York City,
the crisp autumn air, a notion of the impending winter
season, my intoxication further exacerbates my
seclusion
I am alone.
Eight million people inhabit the city and this street now
bare?
With what peculiarity can one compare?
Am I the only man with no place to be?

My predicament lies in my ability to see,
a whitewash town painting so extravagantly
"It's all false!" I shout.
No reply
In the distance a train comes into view
The city has a sound, a muffled rumble
Low, subliminal vibrations
Listen closely, can you hear it?

I think I am going mad

Is that the thought of a madman?

Doesn't the statement in itself imply a level of clarity?

Take a drag; smoke bellows

One less breathe I have

I need a fireplace

I need some whisky in my hand

I need a lover who looks me in the eyes intensely.

Intrepid

Kia Ochun

the noise filtering in
of hot nights and letting go
of solemn murk
where you don't know
which is worse;
the thoughtless numb content
or the thoughts stimulated
to a jiving and lost amount
full of intense rhythm
funneling your passions into a succinct
beam of sound
where you go to pick out your keys
and what you will unlock

A Respite from Rain

Alan Charnock

The fall rain drops a kiss on my lips
between gusts of warm gutter perfume
and garrulous lights on the broadway shout
"get out, get out of the gathering gloom."

Cobblestone mews that crisscross alleys
fraught with rain-slick fire-escapes
wrap me in their antique hush
like a child drowned behind the drapes.

When I'm soaked in rain I remember
how covered in kisses I was when you left
how you made my wrecked nerves sting
and my loneliness is a strange gift:
though it sticks like the grime of this city's sins
it gleams in my heart like a polished thing.

I Won't Tell You

Patricia Gillespie

I want to run into you.
On the street.
And not duck this time.

I want to run into you,
like that time you saw me forget my boss' hard
drives on the L train.
(Thank God those doors stay open so long)

Yes. I want to run into you like that—
but I want you to notice I SEE you this time.
And I want you to see me back:

How well I'm doing.
How slim, my waist.
The fabulous pair of knockers that showed up after
I started taking birth control.
Taking birth control, by the way.
Taking birth control.
Because I have a really attractive boyfriend.
And I won't tell you he has a big pee pee.

I wont tell you because if you meet him, you'll
know.

Yeah.
I want to see you.

I want you to ask questions.
Questions you have answers to
because you've been reading the little about me
that makes print.

I will tell you I have a lit manager.
You will become wildly jealous.
I will tell you he has big clients,
and the last thing on your mind
will be the fact that
all this really means
is that he has no time to call.
Unlike you,
I will fess up to having followed your work.
I will pretend to like it.
Even though you know I hate post modernism,

I will pretend to like it.

And I won't tell you

that I'm disappointed you
turned into a hipster.
I wont tell you
I think grad school's an excuse.
I won't tell you
Everyone thinks it's stupid
That you pretend to hate Lena Dunham
When you're basically Lena Dunham
But skinny, with a receding hairline. And male.

A dirty gust of city wind will blow through my
bangs,
(Freshly cut by the alcoholic neighbor downstairs)
and you'll see me double.
Not double.
Squared?
No, you'll notice me.
And you'll remember the fat girl that followed
you around.
You'll see all the fire, and savvy, and sex that
pours out of her now.
Her, the woman.
Even if she is still a little fat and awkward.

And Jesus Christ,
I want you to be filled with passion and regret.

But you won't be.
And that's okay.

Instead
You'll be filled with the memories I wrote to you
about bad childhoods.
And you'll be scared.
Because I'm out of mine.
Because yours wasn't so bad.
Because you're 26 and still living off your parents.

Yeah, you'll be scared.
You won't say this,
But I'll see it when I'm seeing you.

And I won't tell you
that I am scared, too.
I won't tell you
that I got cancer, that I think I'm fucking up.

I won't tell you,
That for some reason,
Even though
I couldn't be any less attracted to you,
I will always, always love you big and too too deep.

I can swallow all that.
But the kicker?

When I don't tell you
how much it hurt
to figure out
your writing
was bad.

You start to transmit these feelings to different areas of your life. . . Creating stories about people sitting across from you on the L.

~ Brittany Natale

Bushwick Poetry

Inertia

Jonathan Zuckerman

Still. Stuck.
Staying in one position
like a Buddha.
My mind keeps moving forward
To the next station
To the next train
To the walk home
To the people I hopefully won't meet
on my way
To my door
Then I see
the woman sleeping
and the man eating
an apple
with no skin left on it
and my mind stops.
and I'm here again.
Then my mind begins moving forward
once more

Yes and yes man
Linda Penny

Open your eyes, fool. You ain't done yet. Watch your
back. Don't stand there trying to figure out how you got
here. You're here. Now. You have arrived. Alone. Don't
let this shit be the end of you. They're hunters, they are
predators ·

Watch your back, don't back away. Step in close. Own
your opposition just in that moment, in the clutch. He'll
never get a swing off if you get in tight, grab on, you
got the goods. You got the weight, the strength, the
heart. Please dude.

If ya gotta? Drop a hammer on a fucker; fast and hard.

I'm sorry. But in the end, something always dies. It can
be you or them or maybe just a little piece of you, but
something will be gone. Something always dies.
Hey, dude, ya gotta live, right?.

Ovulating on the Full Moon
Julianne Mason

<u>Pt. 1</u>

There are quiet streets that I cannot cross
And way deep down in my stomach my love glows
Long after I've turned this last lamp off
And my mind and my love tangle
And my love glows
I feel this water under my lower abdomen
I want him there
Moving everything
All my hidden stars
Up and out my mouth
I'll send them into his
On little ships of light and the little sails from my torn letter
Paper wings, tiny humming birds
On into his ocean
Which now holds my limp body
And his hands surface
His fingers dry my face
Are these my tears now?
My gift for you to taste

Pt. 2

You lying in my stomach like a black hole and
Every thought is disappearing
I was never anything anyway
Transport me to another universe
Bring me closer to my new self
We are old, we are travelers
Black night of space and my coffee in the morning
I see no difference between them with you, my love
Ceramic galaxy and my morning hands are God
I'll put my lips up to this hot universe and cool her if
I can with a breath of song
Your eyes on a newspaper and mine on your head
The top rim of your glasses makes my new body bend
You are a boy but you are old
And this is the blind siamese twin that occupies your soul
Cannot see itself, it shares a spine and heart
And its four pairs of eyes and double set of brains
Make it difficult and smart
And in this home where your black hole brought me
There are cold tiles beneath my feet
And on your body
And in your tired arms
My tired eyes, my tired skin
Wash themselves and sleep

Pt. 3

What is this love something broad and wide
I could not trap it nor fit the whole of it ever inside
And it slides and moves in and out of me
Fills my heart then makes it glass on a curve of infinity
Slide beside and cradle my mind
Hands that I have three times seen
Hold my neck, put your lips to rest
On my body that is spring
The birds that flutter out from between
My legs have tender baby wings
And I will be their mother
And it will make me old
And though the lines of life will come to my face
I wished on a shooting star that they were yours alone
to hold

Bushwick Poetry

The Lover Transitional

Brittany Natale

The butterflies, the shaky hands, the anticipation. Quick phone calls, late nights, compromise. The tears, the shouting, the heartbreak. It is all necessary stuff. The steady, slow ride up the plateau of passion then the crippling ride down. Hold on, for it is all necessary stuff.

It is always the ruins and ashes after the whole ordeal that fascinate the most. The learning to rebuild yourself after that beloved body is gone and you are left with a ghost—lingering through the halls, and the parks and the rooms and . . . is that him on the train? Can't be. Didn't think so.

That uncomfortable period between the "we" and the "I". That nondescript heavy-hearted feeling that decides to visit you when you lay your head down to sleep or taps you on the shoulder during an afternoon walk on a sunny day. He always liked summer . . .

But time passes and you begin the demystification process. That facade you so carefully built around them starts to crack. All of those extraneous details and adjectives you convinced yourself they were starts to crumble and reveal what was really there. That perfect frame of a person you created in your mind was actually just a figment of the imagination. Your mind coloring in the shades of grey and uncertainty with aspects that it was hoping to find. Persuading yourself that imagination was reality.

You start to transmit these feelings to different areas of your life. Instead of daydreaming during the commute of park picnics and laughing on the roof top you begin to put your thoughts to different use. Creating stories about people sitting across from you on the L. Imagining him to be an heir to a castle in some faraway land where they speak some faraway language.

Maybe she is on her way to pick up her twin girls from school and go home to her architect husband who designed their glass house. Begin to shift those lonely emotions into various compartments of your mind. Redistribute those feelings from the mental "Heartbreak" box into those boxes more deserving. Mitosis of that large body of despair begins to break that mass into tinier, weaker emotions. Time to get off the train, time to transfer to the M. Time to transfer those emotions.

December 1

Amy Richards

I hang paper trees on dead branches.
Inkblots look like living
things: faces, webs, haikus.

How do we turn ourselves back into half
a thing, once the ink's bled through?

Won't listen to empty wine bottles
garbage can music tonight
want to hear soft words above my head
muffled beating in your sweater.

Environmental Science

Gary Estanislao

Folding up my short sleeves tee
Revealing my left arm tattoo
Bar in Bushwick, Brooklyn
Summer ware and crawfish bites
I dress experience with a renaissance-
Ethos always evolving in New York

The movement in this neighborhood
Is about art and food—the privileged
Class politely popping up: a 50 bucks
Men's haircut salon; a Gnostic cafe
In the mixed-use building Loom
Restaurants are traditionalists free forms

A beatnik reprise is what I'm living
Drugged by intellectual sexuality
"The New Secular" according to Brooks
A political style retrospective
Humanizing original poetics to inculcate
The wilderness of the noosphere

Randy
Linda Penny

Randy always talked to me. He really did have the right name. Randy is exactly what he was. Well, not until about fifth grade. He thought he needed to fall in love at least once a month until he turned eighteen because he was going to be a soldier who died in battle like his daddy did.

He would never call his father daddy, always father. That held the respect he felt for him. But I could see the love and the loss in his eyes when he talked about him. That's a daddy, right?

My Randy, how long ago that was.
He had this goofy look on his face whenever he was planning some kind of something, so he never ever got away with it, but that didn't stop him from trying.

He used to put pennies on the train tracks and wait for the train to come along and squish it out smooth and shiny; bye-bye Mr. Lincoln.

He taught me to tell the truth, because I loved him and he deserved the truth. I wanted him to be proud of me. He was my magic.

Every year he'd run over to my house to show off his back to school clothes. September and Easter were new clothes time and he would kinda blend in better, at least for a little while. Then the shoes got old and the shirts got small and his face got sad, lonely for normal, for fitting in.

Maybe it was good in the end that he became a soldier, fit in, had pants his size for more than a few months. Maybe he found some way to do something, somehow. For someone.

We both cried when he left me. I don't know why he had to go. Maybe it was just because he lived his whole life thinking about it. My soldier.

He survived four years in the camps they said. He died in the black pajamas that all the P.O.W.'s wore. His father's son. My magic. My Randy.

How long ago that was.

Malecón

Amy Richards

I picked up the plastic piece of straw
after a cocaína line I never took

tore my shirt into a hundred pieces
wanting to bury my head in it
like I saw an ostrich do on TV once

waved my arms up behind me
hoping you would pull me up
out of my shirt pieces

it was just a beater anyway.

I cried lemon teardrops
as you ate ceviche
asked for more ají

you spooned hot pepper pieces onto raw fish
never realizing this place is a skate park after
dark.

Cantina
Linda Penny

There's a cantina, aways away from Cozumel. Lamp lit
guitar strums; the poor and passionate heroes who
really do define the word. Picnic tables by the parking
lot;

They're of ancient wood bleached winter grey like
brittle bones not yet done baking in the sun. Heat
waving its shivering fingers in the air as it rises off the
hardpan beaten down gravel of the parking spaces,
mating dances; coy smiles on empty faces, *cervezas*.
But the music, there's the fire. We are hot with desperate
hopes, desires, fading dreams, we dance, we sway, give
over another day to lay in hungry arms and dream.

We dream of hope,

We hope we can still dream.

My Palindrome
Patricia Gillespie

I read you All Ways,
Until I can't remember where I am—
Won't you tell me again:
[MadAm, in edeN, I'm AdaM]

Brain spinning silver
In smile lines
Around soft eyes searching—

I have never
Been
More
Naked
Then when you caught me looking.

[Never Odd Nor Even]
I thought I
built myself
into a
Big
Strong
Woman

Tell me
How do you make me feel
So
Damn
Small?

Rodeo Clown,
Your shoulders sway With
so
Much
[War—]
Let me take it from you In a sigh.

Did you know?
 Your body shakes
the same way
 in reverse.

What Can I Give You
Shuang Li

I gave you my love
But that is cheap
Overflowing with the air and water
Reaching every corner of the earth

I gave you my young body
But it has no perfection like a goddess
The skin condition and my flat flat ass
And funny tan lines

So what can I give you in return?
For everything you have done
and haven't

I gave you my time.
Time is solid as fuck
For what is past is past
For what is done is done
Though intangible
For what is gone is gone

I gave you my best years.

The youngest days then the rest my life,
The maturest days then the former of my time,
And I have nothing more to offer you.

What have you given me?
A peaceful mind?

But I would never forget the days when I woke up in
tears and fears
That I had to cut myself once, twice, and endless more
times to calm myself down
And the days I can't even let my face appear out of my
hair

I didn't know how to appreciate myself
Until you taught me .

may baby (maybe)
Arthur Medrano

you were the most hopeful enterprise i'd embarked in.
 you swept me up from the start
  and you wanted.
you wanted what i'd give
 and came back for more.
  consistently pricking the future's mold,
you asked for me to love you.
 i tried, only to be denied later,
  after i'd kissed you.
your absence made me miserable
 but i didn't believe anything that you'd bring was false.
  it was the harsh reality i'd need to face to become the
man

i'd become today.
you came back for awhile, unsettled and emotional -
 detached from all the embraces i gave.
  you withered in your lonely way
   and relied upon others to hold you up,
    when really i had all you'd need.
     you couldn't come to me.
      you were my May baby!

and maybe there's a streak of light somewhere in the

distant future
          once you're out of the fire
          and have ceased screaming.

Off This Rock

Patricia Gillespie

The food cart like a stand-still thurible
outside the business school.
Little brown priest
ain't got much to say about Jesus,
He whispers burning lamb
like a vesper
into the cold autumn morning.

Like in church as a child,
The Call.
My Response:

Thinking
Baby, maybe if I hold you tight enough,
I can keep you
From falling
Off of this rock.

Dishwater,
Light and sweet
All over my second hand coat.
Regular Joes

Dressed up like Freaks, Saviors, Sons
I can't laugh no more,

Thinking
Baby, maybe if you hold me tight enough
You can keep me
From falling
Off of this rock

I think somewhere, back there
I realized I loved this kind of pain,
My knee joints dry
From pavement abuse,
And last nights good cry.

The veins of old men
Screaming silent, outside the liquor store.
A beating neon heart.
I been there.
We grew up hard enough.

Baby, maybe
if we let go true enough
We can get up on off of this rock.

Untitled

Samuel Dibella

Desperate
of the indigenous clay
whisper to violets
I do not fear
And I do not promise.

Under in undinous
an aquatic sun.
holy and the pure
me and I drain

waves as
A forgotten grotto
has its ashes,
a white circle
of past
where the roses bloom.
The present
brandished on violins.

Bushwick Is
Tami O'Neill

Lying naked in a loft

dozing sporadically 'till 4

because you quit your job two months ago

and your freelance gigs fell short.

A woven, ten buck Navajo blanket

from a recent run cross country

hides your skin—as does the sheet

serving as a curtain

from the bustling scene outside:

Mariachi music streaming from shops,

car horns, children chattering.

All coming for the ear at once; both repulsive and
alluring.

Suddenly your smart phone chirps,

sensing the promise of human activity.

Besides, the cat keeps crying;

concerned, hungry, lonesome creature.

So time to climb down from this stupor.

Shower. Spend your hours on laundry, resumes and reading...

maybe a beer or two in the evening.

That's all this town is, really.

On a Tuesday, late in May.

Bushwick Poetry

Bushwick Poetry

Essay: Bushwick The Usual Way

Luke Maguire Armstrong

New York could have been San Francisco. It was almost Portland, and there was a possibility it was going to be Minneapolis, and people kept telling me I should check out Austin.

After four years living in Guatemala, a year in South America, I moseyed up to those two diverging roads Frost got all poetic about. I had never lived in my home country without being either a student or hanging out in Huggies and ultimately decided it was time to return to a place that both felt like home and somewhere foreign—a departure from the settings of five formative post-college years when my gringo-ness was intricate to my identity.

The factors that led into my final decision about which Gringo factory to return to were rather arbitrary, but they led me to arrive in New York at the beginning of October, right when the weather took a dive towards the winter, a few weeks before Sandy.

I spent my first week with a mild case of homelessness which led to a couch of a 78-year-old nudist man in Manhattan, where in the morning I would open my eyes to glimpse his old, wrinkly testicles dangling above me in the apartment's limited space.

He made me dinner and offered me wine and was a big step up from the previous week where the official term for what I was doing was "banging for roof." I arrived in New York with $1,000 and the literature reenforced idea that this was the place that writers went to write and musicians came to sing--as natural as surfing in Costa Rica, binge drinking in Ireland, and smoking hashish in Morocco.

New York HI Hostel was my staging ground for finding an apartment to sublet for a month. But at $60 a night, every night I spent there bit into my meager rent acorn. I could afford a $5 a night locker in the basement of the hostel to keep my stuff in, but after a night couldn't afford a dorm-room bed. I checked out of the hostel and snuck into the basement movie area, where I camped out for two nights while using the WIFI to set up appointments with subletters on Craigslist.

As a fall back, I blanketed New York's Couch Surfing community with requests. At first the only users who responded to my missives replied with detailed over shares and candid TMIs about overwhelming personal situations that prevented them from having a houseguest.

I could sneak into the hostel during the day easily enough with it's busy comings and goings, but if I was going to go out at night, something that a new resident of The City has a burning itch to do, I had to, Plan A: be invited to a sleepover or Plan B: pass the wee hours walking the dark streets or *en garde* on a park bench.

After my second night in the movie room, I needed to get out. A few nights earlier an editor for a travel magazine I wrote for introduced me to a school teacher who had invited me to a Halloween party in Park Slope--the neighborhood that hipsters move to have a career, long-term relationship and/or child.

She was dressed as a female Vulcan and wore a tight green dress. I did not have a costume, so I bought tape at a bodega and taped a paper cup to my chest and a sign that said "First response Pregnancy Test." I told people I was a pregnancy test and no one argued with that. Nineties rock blasted from an iPod, and after a few rum shots I joined everyone in an elaborate circle dance where everyone participated with the rigor of dog inside a butcher's block.

More so than most places, it's the girls who do the picking up in New York City. They run the city with confident laughter and have no problem making their preferences known. Needing someone to invite you to spend the night with them (or in my case, save me from dark walks and park benches) it was not just an exercise of tolerance, but a lesson in moral flexibility we all need if we are going to survive in this world.

"Astrology is so obviously true," she told me as we walked down the brownstone lined streets of Park Slope, on the way to her apartment in Carrol Gardens.

Just because someone asks you what you think, doesn't mean they are asking you to tell the truth.

My night with her was like the twirl in swing dance, part of an already enjoyable time that widens your smile.

The next day I showered with the The Vulcan's shampoo and we sat down at a Thai place in her barrio. We had both had a good time last night, we agreed between delicious bites and sips of her favorite Thai coffee in town.

Even though I was technically homeless at the time, in that morning light I felt like I was right where I was supposed to be. New York was offering me up new friends who smiled and pinched my bicep when I made a joke. Maybe it was because I had spent the last night listening to a Vulcan talk about omens that this seemed like such a good one.

My brunch date walked me to the subway and gave me a tight hug. Back at the hostel I waited like a creeper by the door and slipped in behind a group of Korean students and went to visit my stuff in my locker in the basement. A few subletters responded with phone numbers to set up times to see the rooms and an older gentleman named Bill responded to my message on Couch Surfing, offering me a few days on his couch while I figured things out.

No longer a stowaway in a hostel's dark movie room, (which could just as accurately be called the make-out room); I became roommates to both the man and his balls.

If I had actually read Bill's Couch Surfing profile his abrupt nudity would not have appeared shockingly out of nowhere. This tendency was clearly listed as things likely to happen in his home. When I looked at his profile with his WIFI, I saw that it said explicitly, in several places that one would be hard pressed to catch the man in clothes.

Two days later, I had appointments to see three apartments. The first was a nonstarter. I arrived at the address and no one answered the bell or my calls. The second one was an hour and a half subway ride into a forgotten section of the city. I found the address and man who answered the bell looked like he had dug himself out of a grave for our appointment. He showed me a lightless room that smelled of rats and murder. The windowless wall hid a post apocalyptic neighborhood that seemed to scream "Flee!" My third appointment called me during the showing of Hannibal's home to tell me the room I was to see had just been rented.

On the M train back from a wasted day a sunset burned bright over Manhattan. I vacillated between elation and despair. On one hand, things seemed to be working out wonderfully—here I was, in New York playing my hand. On the flip side, I was broke, jobless, and technically homeless, living under a pair of old balls. New York was not working out.

The thought of spending another exhausting day locating obscure addresses, made me sink. I had left that day with determination not to return until I had a place. Some inner prod moved me to action just as the train stropped. I got out, determined not to get back on the train until I had a place to live.

My plan was vague, and more than a bit naïve, and was decided in an abrupt flash of untested inspiration. As the doors of the M train were about to close, I rushed out, not sure of where I was, and marched down the metal stairs to the street below. The sign said it was the Central Avenue stop.

My plan was to walk around the neighborhood, talking to people on the street, in bars and cafés until I found a place to live.

I would find out later that I was in Bushwick, an up-and-coming neighborhood of mostly Latinos being gentrified with "hipsters" who denied affiliation with hypsterdom despite thick rimmed glasses, flannel, vests, beards and elaborate hats.

A block from the stop I walked into a bike shop. A female and male employee were engaged in conversations with customers. I waited for the male employee, not planning on talking to women, since they might be threatened by some random dude walking the streets asking if they knew of anyone who was subletting a room.

The female employee finished her conversation first and addressed me. She thought she recognized me, "Hey," she said, "how are you doing?"

I told her she had me mistaken, that I had never been in the shop before. I explained to her that I had just moved to New York and was looking for a place to live. She eyed me suspiciously. She owned the shop and had a place across the street. As of that morning, she had decided to rent out a room and told me it was super weird that I would show up right at the time asking about one . . "

We talked back in forth at some length about the possibility of me being a potential serial killer.

Mimicking the mannerisms of the Buddha, I assured her I had never murdered so much as a single person. I admitted to no one that yes, as a child, I had blown up a few frogs with fire crackers, but that I deeply regretted this and what 9 year old boy in North Dakota hadn't conducted such experiments?

"Denying that you are a serial killer," she pointed out, "is exactly what a serial killer would do."

"But," I countered, "It is also certainly something that a non-serial would naturally do."

We were at a stalemate, so I played a trump card. On her laptop I Googled an interview I had done with Christina Aumanpour about a malnourished infant center that I had opened and run in Guatemala.

She introduced herself as KT and invited a female customer with a black leather jacket to come with us. She was German, and presumably could take me if the video had been some sort of serial killer's ploy.

Inside KT offered me a Brooklyn Lager. She and her one-year-old daughter lived in the apartment. She had just separated with the baby daddy and needed to sublet out the former office to make ends meet.

The next day, I moved in with KT, her daughter, and their two black cats--Karl and an identical one whose named I've since forgotten (so clearly not as memorable as Karl).

Over the next two months Bushwick became my neighborhood, their bars my taverns and New York my home. When I wrote, Karl would sit on my keyboard and twitch his tail. I lived there with someone who treated me like a rockstar, and never ceased when I practiced my guitar to demand I sing for her Old McDonald. She excelled at the EIEIOs and blurted them out with a seriousness few musicians have.

New York City has a literal vastness of figurative potential, which on a good day is great, but on a bad day can make you feel like drowning. You need an anchor. I found Bushwick a lighthouse with a welcoming glow. Nights at bars often led to rooftop jamming sessions, where people passed smokes and beers and everyone joined in the song. During the day you run into the same people, hispanic, and hipster, and in my case even two brothers from North Dakota, my home state, showed up with a nightly predictability at my favorite bar.

Whatever brought me to New York is not what keeps me here, since I still don't know how anyone gets any substantial writing done in a city that keeps you up all night.

There is a stereotype that persists that New Yorkers are harsh and unfriendly. That's maybe true if you don't veer off the tourist streets. But inside apartments, cafés and taverns, they are some of the warmest, most accepting people out there. They are in a hurry, of course, but so is everyone faced with the enormity of The City's endless offerings of all things you're into.

We don't always know where a road will take us or who will be seated at our midnight tables. My midnight table here contains supportive souls who lead and challenge by artistic and personal example.

It was not till now, a year later, that I've written an account of the thin wire I walked in the beginning, when New York was still a skyline of question marks.At the time I did not let anyone know, certainly not my friends and acquaintances who lived in New York and might have offered me a place to crash. Some of that had to do with plain old fashion pride that New York can humble. I left a swell life in a city I was fanatic about and could not bring myself to even muse about the possibility that I might have made a mistake.

New York, Bushwick specifically, ended up being what I hoped it could be at a time when I needed it to be and I'll always have a lovely word to say about her for that.

More essays at TravelWriteSing.com

Acknowledgments

There is a lot of thanks to go around for this book. Thanks to you the reader, for getting all the way to page 89. Unless you cheated and are for some reason reading this before the poetry. Please, go back and read the poetry first.

I want to thank Bushwick, and the people who helped made that happen for me, Jennifer Martinez, Andrew Davis, Don Pepito del Diablo, KT Higgins, Matt Stabile. The taco stand. Thanks to Candice Walsh and Alan Charnock for the wonderful copy editing. Gracias to Ada Badada for your hula hooping. Thanks to Steven and the Goodbye Blue Monday. Thanks to Pearls Social Billy Club and god bless the Gotham City Lounge for your $3/shot of whiskey and PBR combo.

Made in the USA
Columbia, SC
04 June 2021